# VLADIMIR LENIN'S SOVIET UNION

## Biography for Kids 9-12

## Children's Biography Books

**BABY PROFESSOR**
EDUCATION KIDS

Speedy Publishing LLC

40 E. Main St. #1156

Newark, DE 19711

www.speedypublishing.com

Copyright 2017

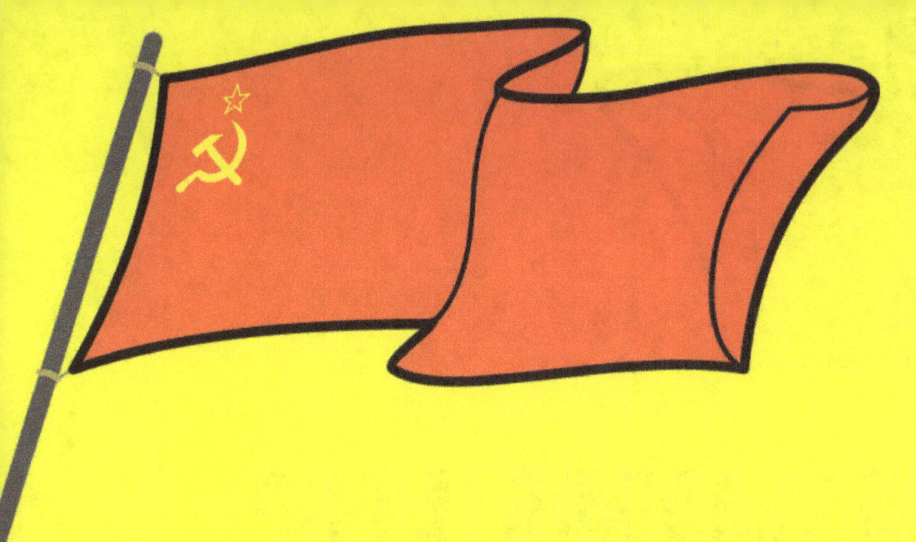

In this book, we're going to talk about the life of revolutionary Vladimir Lenin. So, let's get right to it!

# WHO WAS VLADIMIR LENIN?

Vladimir Ilich Ulyanov, known simply as Lenin, was the head of the Communist Party in Russia and he led the Bolshevik Revolution in 1917. He was also the first leader of the Soviet Union from 1917 to 1924.

ВАМ ВЫПАЛА ВЕЛИКАЯ
ЧЕСТЬ С ОРУЖИЕМ В
ЗАЩИЩАТЬ СВЯТЫЕ ИД
В.И.
Monument of Vladimir Lenin

# LENIN'S EARLY LIFE

Lenin's birthplace was Simbirsk, Russia and he was born in April of 1870. He came from an educated family and his father's profession was teaching. Lenin was studious and in addition to his academic studies he loved being outdoors and winning at chess.

However, things changed in Lenin's life when he was sixteen years of age. His father passed away suddenly. Lenin's attitude toward life completely changed. He didn't understand why God had taken his father away from him. He proclaimed that he was an atheist and no longer believed in God. He refused to attend the Russian Orthodox parish where he had worshipped before.

Russian Orthodox Church

Russian Imperial Family 1913

One year after the death of their father, Lenin's brother Sacha became a revolutionary. At that time, Russia was ruled by a monarch called the Tsar. Sacha and the others in his revolutionary group participated in a plot to assassinate the Tsar.

The plot was discovered by the government, and Sacha was caught and put to death by execution. Now Lenin had lost both his father and his older brother and he was driven by an anger that was more violent than before.

НТЕРН ПРО

Russian Revolution

# LENIN BECOMES A REVOLUTIONARY

Despite his emotional turmoil, Lenin kept up with his studies. He attended the Kazan University in Tatarstan, Russia and while there he became interested in pursuing politics, especially the revolutionary aspect of politics.

He began reading and studying the works of the radical Prussian philosopher, Karl Marx. Marx had written a book in 1848 called the "The Communist Manifesto." This book calls for workers to destroy the principles of capitalism, abandon socialism, and instead create a revolution based on the tenets of communism.

Karl Marx

Kazan

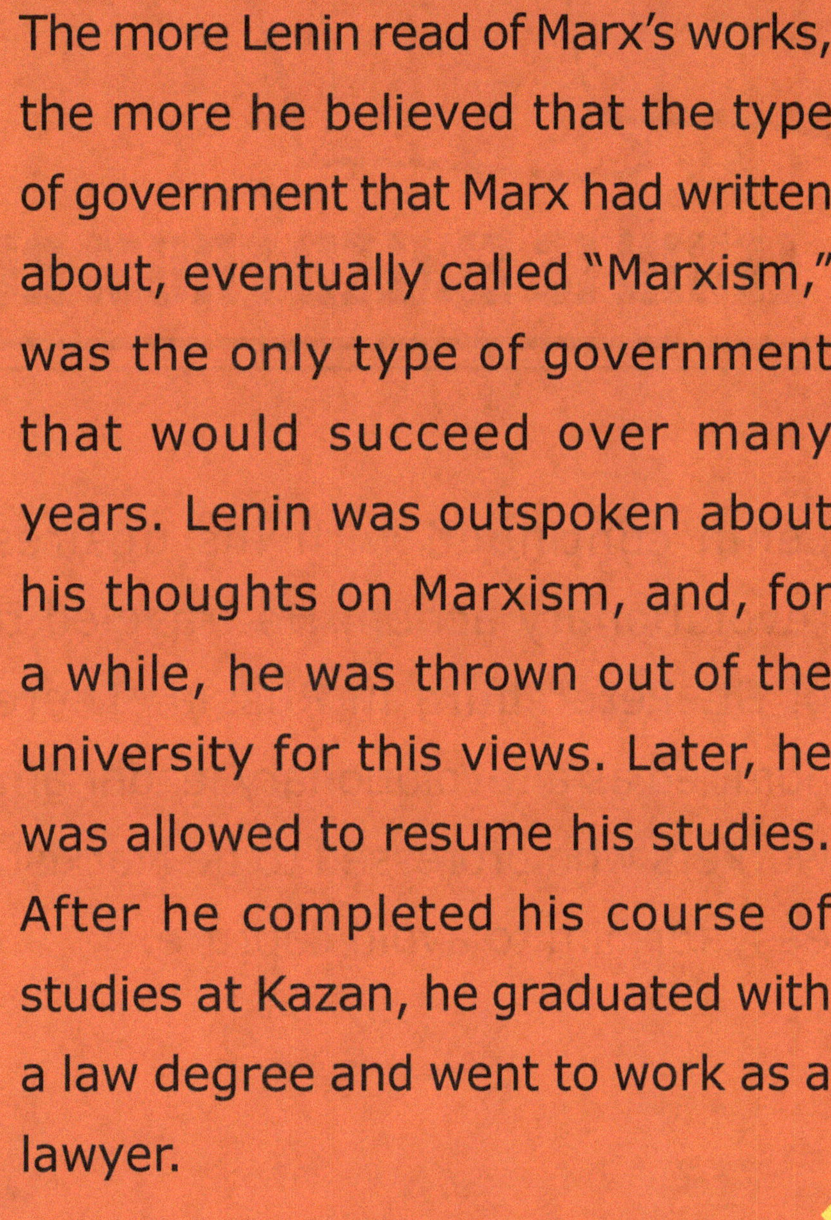

The more Lenin read of Marx's works, the more he believed that the type of government that Marx had written about, eventually called "Marxism," was the only type of government that would succeed over many years. Lenin was outspoken about his thoughts on Marxism, and, for a while, he was thrown out of the university for this views. Later, he was allowed to resume his studies. After he completed his course of studies at Kazan, he graduated with a law degree and went to work as a lawyer.

# LENIN IS EXILED FROM RUSSIA

Lenin continued with his desires to take revolutionary action. He traveled to the city of St. Petersburg in Russia. There, he was admired as a revolutionary leader among other workers who professed to be Marxist. It wasn't easy for him to avoid capture.

St. Petersburg, Russia

Bolsheviks

He constantly had to hide from officials of the government. Spies working for the government were everywhere and it was difficult to know who he could trust. As Lenin's leadership grew, he founded his own group of Marxist workers. He called them the Bolsheviks.

Lenin's plans to put revolution into practice were delayed when he was caught in 1897. He was sent to Siberia, an area of Russia that is a frozen wasteland. He returned from Siberia in three years, however, the government police were still watching his every move. He was exiled from St. Petersburg and traveled to Western Europe while he waited for the proper time to take action. While he was there, he authored papers on communism.

St Petersburg

World War 1
ICHARD ASSMANN
1919

# THE BEGINNING OF WORLD WAR I

In 1914, the first World War began. At this time, Russia was still under the leadership of the Tsar. Millions of laborers and peasants in Russia were drafted into the army. The conditions were beyond horrible. They had been given no training and were forced to fight with little or no food. Sometimes they had to fight without wearing shoes or carrying any weapons. Throughout the war, millions of these men were killed. The Russian people had had enough. They were ready to start the revolution.

# THE FEBRUARY REVOLUTION

The revolution broke out in March 8 of 1917, but the calendar was different in Russia, so it was called the February Revolution. The Tsar was removed from his throne and a temporary government, called the Provisional Government, was put into place. With help from the German government, Lenin traveled back to his homeland.

February Revolution

Vladimir Lenin

He became very vocal in speaking against this temporary government. He proclaimed that it wasn't any better than the government run by the Tsar had been. He wanted to install a government that was run by the people and that operated under the principles of communism.

# BOLSHEVIK REVOLUTION

In October of that same year, Lenin and his group of Bolsheviks overthrew the government. This event was called the Bolshevik Revolution and is sometimes referred to as the October Revolution. Lenin established the new government and became its leader. It was called the Soviet Republic.

October Revolution

Soviet Republic Monument

# LENIN BECOMES SOVIET UNION LEADER

Once Lenin was in charge, he began to make many changes. He made peace with Germany since they had helped him to gain admittance back into Russia. The Soviet Republic didn't continue to fight in World War I. The Germans were pleased with this response. This had been their goal when they helped him. He also seized land from wealthy landowners and divided it into sections so that it would belong to the workers and peasants as part of the principles of communism.

# RUSSIAN CIVIL WAR

Not everyone in Russia was pleased with the Bolshevik philosophy. Many were opposed to their teachings and were unhappy with the changes. During the first few years he was in power, Lenin battled against this opposition in a civil war. Lenin was a ruthless, brutal leader. He killed anyone who spoke out against his beliefs and the new government.

The Red Army, Civil War

He drafted the peasants into his armed forces and took food from their farms to feed the army. This war of Russian against Russian destroyed what was left of the country's economy. Millions of people had no food and died of starvation. His leadership was no different than the Tsar's earlier leadership.

During this time, he established a policy called War Communism. This policy meant that the government essentially owned everything in the country. Individuals couldn't own anything of their own. This meant that soldiers could seize anything that they needed from private citizens.

Kolchak Armies

Bolsheviks

Once the war was over and the Bolsheviks were victorious, the country was in shambles. In order to revive the economy, Lenin established a New Economic Policy. Surprisingly, under this new policy he allowed some private businesses and farms, a form of capitalism under the mask of communism.

Now that his new regime had no one fighting to oppose it, Lenin named the new country "The Soviet Union" in 1922. It was the first country to have a system of government that was conducted under a communist philosophy.

The Soviet Union Monument

Lenin's Mausoleum

# ASSASSINATION ATTEMPT AND DEATH

In 1918, while Lenin had been giving a talk at a factory, a woman named Fanny Kaplan shot him three times with a revolver. She wanted to kill Lenin because she felt that he had been a traitor to the true spirit of the revolution. Lenin barely survived, but his health never recovered. Beginning in 1922, he started to have strokes and he passed away from a stroke in January of 1924.

# LEGACY

Lenin was one of the most powerful as well as one of the most brutal leaders during the 20th century. History will remember his ideas on Marxism as well as his advocacy of communism. His philosophy is known today as Leninism. For many years, Lenin was thought of as a great leader, but since the Soviet Union was dissolved in 1991, the people in the countries that were once the Soviet Union have changed their thinking. Today, thousands of statues of Vladimir Lenin have been toppled.

Statue of Vladimir Lenin

Monument of Vladimir Lenin

# INTERESTING FACTS ABOUT LENIN

The city where Lenin was born was named Ulyanovsk to honor him.

In 1922, he authored a document called Testament.

In it he proclaimed that Joseph Stalin should not be allowed to keep his position in the government. However, it was too late. Stalin took over the government after Lenin died. He was just as brutal as Lenin.

Vladimir Lenin and Joseph Stalin

Lena River

He adopted the name "Lenin" around 1901. It's likely that this alias derived from the name of the River Lena. This river was located near the area where he lived in Siberia for three years.

Lenin was married. He wed a woman revolutionary by the name of Nadya Krupskaya in 1898.

Vladimir Lenin Statue at Svobody Square

In 1900, Lenin established and ran a newspaper that supported communist beliefs. It was called Iskra.

Now you know more about the life of Vladimir Lenin and his influence in the Soviet Union. You can find more Biography books from Baby Professor by searching the website of your favorite book retailer.

Visit
BABY PROFESSOR
EDUCATION KIDS
www.BabyProfessorBooks.com
to download Free Baby Professor eBooks
and view our catalog of new and exciting
Children's Books